WORDS OF
JESUS

LOVING & UNDERSTANDING THE BEATITUDES

WORDS OF JESUS

LOVING & UNDERSTANDING THE BEATITUDES

GANEL-LYN CONDIE

CFI
An imprint of Cedar Fort, Inc.
Springville, Utah

Paperback ISBN 13: 978-1-4621-4721-2
eBook ISBN 13: 978-1-4621-4833-2

Published by CFI, an imprint of Cedar Fort, Inc.
2373 W. 700 S., Suite 100, Springville, UT 84663
Distributed by Cedar Fort, Inc., www.cedarfort.com

Library of Congress Cataloging Number: 2024936344

Cover design by Shawnda Craig
Cover design © 2024 Cedar Fort, Inc.

Printed in the United States of America
10 9 8 7 6 5 4 3 2 1
Printed on acid-free paper

Dedicated to my friend and word weaver, Boyd Matheson.
Thank you for speaking the words of Jesus
when the world needs them most.

Contents

Introduction

I'm grateful you're reading this, especially if you never read the introduction in books. I want to explain why I wrote this book. I hope it enriches your reading.

Honestly, I wasn't sure there was another book in me. I had shattered my wrist in fifty-two places and was recovering. Then one day, while doing my daily scripture study, I found myself distracted. I kept picking up my phone and scrolling and adding tasks to my to-do list. I stopped and put my phone down, but the cycle continued. I offered a simple prayer: "Father, help me to focus and feel Thy Spirit while I read just a few verses of scripture today." As soon as I said "amen," the Spirit prompted me with a thought—it was actually more like a question. *What if I only had one chapter of scriptures to read or study? What would God want me to focus on? What would be most important to understand?* Almost immediately, the answer came to my mind's eye. It was almost too obvious. *Why hadn't I considered it before?*

The answer comes to each of us in two different books of scripture. Both the New Testament and the Book of Mormon spotlight Jesus's teachings. His special sermon was given on both continents. The Savior gave the Sermon on the Mount, also known as the Beatitudes, to His disciples in the Holy Land and to the Saints on the American continent after His Resurrection. In it, we learn how to develop a spiritual character to become more like Jesus.

My most powerful impression came next. As I pondered further, I considered, *What might Jesus teach when He comes again? Is it possible that Jesus's mortal and Nephite ministries signal to all of us exactly what He will teach us when He ministers to us during the Second Coming?*

If the Savior taught the same principles during His mortal and resurrected ministries, and possibly will teach them at His Second Coming, how clearly do I understand and apply these poignant teachings? Questions open the door to personal revelation. I want to ask you the same question the Spirit directed to me that day. Do you have a clear internal integration of Jesus's teachings from His sermons?

If the Savior teaches the Beatitudes again, I want to be ready. Like preparing for a Sunday School lesson, I want to be able to engage, comment, and share insights about these cherished teachings.

To improve the impact of scripture study, I ask why God included what He did in the records. Many stories and details have made it into our canonized scriptures, and countless experiences have been edited out of the records. As a lifelong student of the scriptures, I can get complacent. I sometimes take for granted that printed and digital copies are always close by.

That morning I felt like heaven gave me a wake-up call: do more to study, ponder, and apply the very personal and specific teachings of Jesus. There are but a few selections where the teachings aren't a revelatory excerpt but instead a direct record of what Deity taught. These verses are the words God. Powerful are the words of the Beatitudes because they are a record of what Jesus said.

"Ponder the path of thy feet and let all thy ways be established" (Proverbs 4:26). The glorious moment when the Savior returns will be filled with awe and wonder. I hope you will begin today to see how clearly Jesus loves you. He wants a personal relationship with you. There is no evidence that the first family home evening lesson taught by the Savior will be taken from the Sermon on the Mount. But I hope this small book will help you get ready for whatever it may look like. It will provide both historical and modern insights and a place for you to reflect and apply what you feel and learn along the way. I hope that as you work your way through each of the Beatitudes, you will feel Jesus personally teaching you with His words.

One night our family was watching the popular Bible series, *The Chosen*, and the purpose of this book was validated. One of the reasons for the success of this film production is the accessibility of the

Savior. We see ourselves in the scriptures walking with Jesus. Parables, miracles, and His teachings come alive. That is my prayer for this book. I want this information to not overwhelm you but inspire you to walk more personally with Jesus. I invite you to see yourself in the scriptures and in the teachings. Maybe even in the many miracles.

*   *   *

Before we finish the introduction, I'd like to share a few facts that will enhance your study of the Beatitudes.

Beatitudes is Latin for "as blessed or state of joy."[1] These promised blessings, also known as the Sermon on the Mount, are Jesus's beloved teachings to Christians. Because of an additional record, it is especially important for baptized members of The Church of Jesus Christ of Latter-day Saints. The resurrected Lord taught it in the book of Matthew as well as in the Western Hemisphere to the Nephites and the Lamanites found in 3 Nephi 12–14. The Beatitudes describe qualities, invite experiences, and encourage characteristics to help us become more spiritually mature. When God commands us in anything, there is a complementing blessing. He is a god of laws.

Why study the commandments found in the Beatitudes? As we integrate a deeper understanding of Jesus's teaching and live the principles taught in His sermons, we will be blessed with joy, love, and greater peace. Basically, God promises us that it is worth our study and effort to better understand Jesus's profound and simple teachings.

There are some differences between the New Testament account in Matthew 5 and the Book of Mormon version. The Book of Mormon sermon has two new "beatitudes" (see 3 Nephi 12:1–2) not found in the Bible. The Joseph Smith Translation of the Bible (JST) has incorporated these additions. Consider the Book of Mormon as a complement to the Bible. With both records, we have a greater opportunity to learn *of* Jesus and learn *from* Jesus. While both records are of exceptional value, in this book we will study the Book of Mormon version of the Beatitudes.

---

1. https://www.vocabulary.com/dictionary/beatitude#:~:text=The%20noun%20
beatitude%20refers%20to,is%20often%20linked%20to%20beatitude.

I love making Jesus the focus of my studies, and I hope you also see the value in it. Elder James W. McConkie III of the Quorum of the Seventy shared how as a mission president in the Czech/Slovak Mission, he and his wife made Jesus the focus for their missionaries and family:

> Spending time with Jesus in the scriptures changed everything. We gained a deeper appreciation for who He was and what was important to Him. Together we considered how He taught, what He taught, the ways He showed love, what He did to bless and serve, His miracles, how He responded to betrayal, what He did with difficult human emotions, His titles and names, how He listened, how He resolved conflict, the world He lived in, His parables, how He encouraged unity and kindness, His capacity to forgive and to heal, His sermons, His prayers, His atoning sacrifice, His Resurrection, His gospel.[2]

Because of this focused study of the Savior, the McConkies and their missionaries developed an appreciation and trust of the Lord that comes from understanding His words. As you study Jesus's two special sermons, I pray you come to understand His way, His character, and, most important, His love for you.

I am excited to start this study. I love the scriptures and having conversations about how they apply to our real life. We will study each beatitude one at a time and, with the Spirit, we will learn together. The expectation isn't to become a super scriptural expert, but at the end of this study, I pray you better understand how much Jesus loves you, believe He wants to walk with you, and accept the invitation to become more like Him. Bringing this book to you has been a journey. I hope my words and most importantly the words of Jesus help you love and better understand your own personal journey on the road to Emmaus.

And I look forward to sitting next to you at some future gathering when you might raise your hand and share a vulnerable experience from learning and being blessed by the Beatitudes. So, let's put down our cell phones and get started.

---

2. James W. McConkie III, "And They Sought to See Jesus Who He Was," *Liahona*, November 2022, 46.

1

BLESSED ARE THEY

Who Give Heed

---

*Blessed are ye if ye shall give heed unto the
words of these twelve whom I have chosen
from among you to minister unto you,
and to be your servants.*

—3 NEPHI 12:1

As we begin our personal Book of Mormon journey through the Beatitudes, I hope you feel excitement and anticipation to have more Jesus in your life. Consider the context and content of this book as your very own special *Come, Follow Me* lesson with the Savior:

> And it came to pass that when Jesus had spoken these words unto Nephi, and to those who had been called, . . . and behold, he stretched forth his hand unto the multitude, and cried unto [you]. (3 Nephi 12:1)

When the resurrected Savior preached the Beatitudes on the American continent, He had organized the Church in the Americas, taught His leaders, and set apart Nephi and the Twelve Apostles to perform ordinances. The Savior is now crying out for the people to listen and learn what He knows will help them after He is gone. His counsel was first for the Nephites at the gathering outside the temple at Bountiful but also for us, the future readers, to find the kingdom of God and become like Him. The Beatitudes are like a compass that will help you find that kingdom.

The first promised blessing from the Savior is, **"Blessed are ye if ye shall give heed unto the words"** (3 Nephi 12:1). The invitation is to give heed to the servants of God, which is a key to opening the door to future learning and progression. Jesus is encouraging obedience and willingness. Note the intended audience for this sermon: those who were baptized and those intending to be baptized. That means it is for all of us.

The ability to *give heed* is more than just listening to a good sermon or making a comment in class. *Heeding* is hearing and acting on that knowledge. To *heed* is to build on what you learn and feel. The Savior knew He would soon leave the people, and they would need essential steps to return to the Father. These teachings are the divine guideposts needed to learn and then leap into action.

When we heed God's servants, we heed God. Modern-day scripture declares, "What I the Lord have spoken, I have spoken, and I excuse not myself; and though the heavens and the earth pass away, my word shall not pass away, but shall all be fulfilled, whether by mine own voice or by the voice of my servants, it is the same" (Doctrine and Covenants 1:38). Jesus's first invitation is about our willingness to *give heed* to His teachings. By doing so, you lay the groundwork for making and keeping covenants and for achieving eternal happiness.

A powerful example of this kind of faith in action comes from another Book of Mormon story that involves the prophet Alma from King Noah's court. He heeds a servant of God, Abinadi, who testifies to the court and calls the wicked priests to repentance. Alma does exactly what Jesus invites each of us to do in the first beatitude. He exercises humility, believes on God's words, and then acts. Alma repents of his sins, but he doesn't stop there. This ex-member of the wicked King Noah's court then begins to secretly share his beliefs with the Nephites. Alma tells the people about his faith in Jesus and invites them to also repent and be baptized.

Alma then escapes from King Noah's court and hides from his servants for many days. While he hides, Alma writes down what the prophet Abinadi taught. He then goes to the Nephites secretly and teaches them Abinadi's message. Alma tells the people to have faith in Jesus Christ and repent. He hides near a pool called the Waters of Mormon and continues to teach the people. And then those who believe his teachings, which are God's words, are baptized. Eventually, Alma and an additional 204 people are baptized into the Church of Christ. All of this happens because one person listened, learned, humbled himself, believed, and made a decision to change (see Mosiah 18).

Heeding is a powerful act of faith. It is literally faith in action. As we listen, learn, and leave behind our sins, we are blessed, especially if our heeding leads to making covenants with God. "Therefore blessed are ye if ye shall believe in me" (3 Nephi 12:21).

* * *

The covenant path begins with being baptized and receiving the Holy Ghost, but it does not end there. Temple covenants such as those found in the endowment and initiatory open us up to receive more of God's power in our daily lives.

I believe that God does not panic when we step off the covenant path. He is like a patient hen constantly inviting and lovingly gathering her chicks. There is no panic in His outstretched wings. I try to remind myself of this truth when people I love take detours—sometimes very long detours—in making and keeping covenants. I have been inspired by people close to me who, for a time, do *not heed* but then with great humility and effort take the steps back to the path.

My friend Karen[1] has been a great example of heeding. After taking some time away from the Church, she found her way back. Now as a mother of young children, Karen knows what her *why* was for returning—she wanted community. After a few years of developing connections with her ward family, she knew that the time had come to expand her *why*. A societal focus had been a great reason to

---

1. Name has been changed.

come back, but to sustain her conversion, she needed a more personal focus on worship and covenant keeping.

Karen heard the words of President Russell M. Nelson, who, following his ordination as President of the Church in January 2018, said, "Now, to each member of the Church I say: Keep on the covenant path. Your commitment to follow the Savior by making covenants with Him and then keeping those covenants will open the door to every spiritual blessing and privilege available to men, women and children everywhere."[2]

It was an invitation to all of God's children to make and keep covenants. Karen then listened to President Nelson's October 2018 general conference address in which he said:

> My dear brothers and sisters, the assaults of the adversary are increasing exponentially, in intensity and in variety. Our need to be in the temple on a regular basis has never been greater. I plead with you to take a prayerful look at how you spend your time. Invest time in your future and in that of your family. If you have reasonable access to a temple, I urge you to find a way to make an appointment regularly with the Lord—to be in His holy house— then keep that appointment with exactness and joy.[3]

Karen not only heard the prophet's counsel but acted. She heeded. At first, she decided to start reading the Book of Mormon and pondered on the prophet's teaching about the temple. President Nelson had clearly prophesied that there never has been a greater need to be in the temple, on a regular basis, than now. At the time, Karen was not endowed and was overwhelmed at the thought of the steps required to get there. We talked about how she might act on this prophetic invitation. After some time, we decided that Karen could take scriptures and a journal and visit the Draper Utah Temple. In this temple, like in many other temples, there is a main waiting area and also a smaller,

---

2. Sydney Walker, "Invitations President Nelson has given since he became President of the Church," *Church News*, October 29, 2023.

3. Russell M. Nelson, "Becoming Exemplary Latter-day Saints," *Liahona*, November 2019, 114.

quieter waiting area with a couch and beautiful artwork. We scheduled a day to go together. Karen was nervous about going. Questions about worthiness and flawlessness were swimming in her mind.

On the appointed day, we took our journals and scriptures and made our way through the front door of that magnificent house of the Lord. We walked past the main front lobby seating and pushed through the door to the smaller, quieter waiting room. The artwork felt like a personal signal from God that Karen indeed belonged in His house. The depiction of the woman at the well was a perfect reminder of the tender mercies our Heavenly Parents send to their children when they are willing, trying, and seeking. We sat and read, journaled, and prayed. It was a profound experience because Karen felt so comfortable. She belonged in God's temple. After that day, she didn't need anyone to go with her. Karen scheduled times on her calendar to "be in the temple" just like the prophet had invited all of us to do.

Over time Karen read the Book of Mormon, met with her bishop, and started taking steps toward receiving her own endowment. Friends and family gathered at the temple to support and rejoice with Karen when she made covenants with God.

Karen's example of heeding is inspiring. The details of why and how someone walks away are overshadowed with the joy of their eventual return.

In the years since Karen's willingness to visit that temple waiting room with her journal, I have watched her continue to foster a deeper relationship with the temple and thus with God. Life hasn't been perfect, but because of her willingness to heed, she has had access to greater priesthood power to navigate the hard and the unexpected parts of life.

We are often stopped from heeding because of our past, our mistakes, or our fears. We sometimes think that we have made too many mistakes to make our way back. As Elder Jeffrey R. Holland of the Quorum of the Twelve testified:

> However late you think you are, however many chances you think you have missed, however many mistakes you feel you have made or talents you think you don't have, or however far from home

and family and God you feel you have traveled, I testify that you have not traveled beyond the reach of divine love. It is not possible for you to sink lower than the infinite light of Christ's Atonement shines.[4]

Don't let past mistakes make you think that prophetic invitations and teachings are intended for everyone else but not for you. You are loved and needed. Commandments and invitations are about a relationship for everyone. God is asking all of His children to heed not because He is power hungry but because He truly loves you. All He asks is for our willing heart. When we give our will, we are in place to receive more.

The next time you are listening to a general conference and the teachings from the pulpit feel overwhelming or triggering, I hope you will think of Alma and my friend Karen. Give *heed* to what you hear. Don't get overwhelmed. Just take one step forward in faith, and God will meet you there. Whatever God asks from His children, He always gives back a hundred-fold.

POINTS TO PONDER

What are five of the most recent invitations from our prophet?

1. _____

   _____

2. _____

   _____

3. _____

   _____

---

4. Jeffrey R. Holland, "The Laborers in the Vineyard," *Liahona*, May 2012, 33.

4. _____

_____

5. _____

_____

What invitation or prophecy felt important for your personal spiritual momentum? Journal about what you are going to heed.

_____

_____

_____

_____

_____

_____

_____

_____

_____

_____

What are two acts of faith you can perform this week?

_____

_____

_____

_____

_____

_____

_____

_____

_____

_____

_____

_____

_____

2

BLESSED ARE THEY

Who Believe and Are Baptized

And again, more blessed are they who shall believe in your words because that ye shall testify that ye have seen me, and that ye know that I am. Yea, blessed are they who shall believe in your words, and come down into the depths of humility and be baptized, for they shall be visited with fire and with the Holy Ghost, and shall receive a remission of their sins.

—3 NEPHI 12:2

How did you do with the first beatitude? In some ways, the next blessing builds on the first. Hopefully the wheels are beginning to turn and you are settling into a cozy seat, learning at the feet of the Savior as you study His sermon.

After heeding, you are invited to *believe*. Belief may feel somewhat abstract. When a word feels intangible, it is helpful to consider words that could be used in its place. What comes to mind when you think about believing? To *believe* is more than just to have faith in something. Belief feels like trusting, pondering, and then becoming more certain of something. Belief is expansive and less constraining. Sometimes we throw around how much we *know* in the gospel. Ward members stand up in fast and testimony meeting and make statements such as, "I know [fill in the blank] is true." But what if we shared more testimonies of *belief,* such as, "I believe the Church is true"?

The blessing in this verse starts with belief and leads to fruits of faith, specifically that of baptism and receiving the gift of the Holy Ghost. We learn that those "**who shall believe in your words . . . come down into the depths of humility and be baptized**, for they shall be visited with fire and with the Holy Ghost (3 Nephi 12:2; emphasis added). In this powerful portion of the sermon, Jesus teaches His disciples that belief comes after humility, which then moves the wheel of faith forward. Humility opens the gate wider to learning more from God. It is believing and then being willing to make a commitment. The first verse of 3 Nephi 12 teaches us to heed. Verse 2 emphasizes the importance of humility and belief as a precursor to baptism and receiving the gift of the Holy Ghost. What is the promised blessing? You "shall receive a remission of [your] sins."

Why are baptism and the gift of the Holy Ghost so important? Jesus taught the importance of baptism by example. At the age of thirty, Jesus of Nazareth left His home and walked in the wilderness to find His relative John the Baptist. John recognized Jesus as the Savior and declared, "Behold the Lamb of God, which taketh away the sin of the world" (John 1:29). Jesus didn't just *teach* humility; He lived this specific characteristic. He humbly asked John to baptize Him. John was confused, perhaps thinking that the sole purpose of baptism is to wash away sins. Since Jesus had never sinned, John asked why a holy and perfect person like Jesus needed repentance and baptism.

> But John forbad him, saying, I have need to be baptized of thee, and comest thou to me? And Jesus answering said unto him, Suffer it to be so now: for thus it becometh us to fulfil all righteousness. Then he suffered him. (Matthew 3:14–15)

John and Jesus then walked together into the Jordan River, where John baptized Jesus by immersion. When Jesus came out of the water, the heavens opened, and a dove that represented the Spirit of God descended. A voice from heaven said, "This is my beloved Son, in whom I am well pleased" (Matthew 3:17). Can you imagine what a beautiful baptism that was to attend? Maybe we attended as heavenly witnesses. I don't know what the angel choirs may have sung on that glorious day or who may have watched the sacred event from the shoreline. The power of pondering invites us to put ourselves in those special scenes from long ago. Consider what it must have been like to gaze out at the Savior, humbly being baptized, teaching us by example.

Maybe you have heard people say that Jesus didn't need to get baptized. Yes, He was perfect and without sin, but His mission was to show us how to have a relationship with God. And God is no respecter of persons. He wanted to teach us that covenants and commandments are about our connection with God. Jesus showed us what a willing and obedient heart looks like. His baptism reinforces how important a relationship with His Father was and how covenant making is about connection with heaven. Christ came to earth to say, "Come, follow me," because He knew the path on which to walk. And this verse shows the first steps on our mortal journey: belief, baptism, and the Holy Ghost.

* * *

Don't you love hearing those inspiring mission stories about faithful missionaries knocking on a random door, finding a willing investigator, teaching the truths of the gospel, and witnessing the changes that come when someone chooses to repent and enters the waters of baptism? Isn't it powerful to hear how all the previous decisions and detours prepare an investigator to receive a witness from the Spirit and believe?

But what about the belief and baptism of an eight-year-old? It may be tempting to dismiss the miracle of a Primary child, raised in a gospel-centered home, who decides to enter the waters of baptism. Why do we discount this act of heeding and belief? We shouldn't. The scriptures teach otherwise:

And said, Verily I say unto you, except ye be converted, and become as little children, ye shall not enter into the kingdom of heaven. Whosoever therefore shall humble himself as this little child, the same is greatest in the kingdom of heaven. (Matthew 18:3–4)

Don't be so quick to minimize the faith and force of one eight-year-old who courageously believes. God is inviting us, no matter our age, to become like a little child.

If you were baptized at the age of eight, what do you remember from that day? I remember many details from my special day in a Sacramento, California, chapel in February 1979. My parents had divorced, and my mom was remarried. My stepfather, Daddy Jim, had joined the Church as an adult. My father, Daddy Dan, joined the Church as a young child after his mother, my Grandma Esther, fed the missionaries and listened to the discussions. I was grateful for adults who had come before me and helped foster my young faith and belief.

I remember standing in many fast and testimony sacrament meetings sharing my childlike faith through tears. My belief was simple. I recall some of the Primary children teasing me because they didn't understand why I cried every time I shared my unpretentious witness. Looking back on eight-year-old Ganel-Lyn, it is clear now why I always got so emotional. It was the personal witness of the Spirit. Every time it overwhelmed my little girl's heart, the waterworks would start. Crying isn't the only way you may feel the Holy Ghost near. Some feel it through joy, clarity, or knowledge. But for me personally, the language of the Spirit is often accompanied by tears.

I don't remember a lot that led up to my special baptism day. But I do remember some key moments of the day. I asked Daddy Jim to baptize me and Daddy Dan to confirm me. I had to be baptized three times due to a floating foot that kept rising to the top. After all of the re-baptizing, the thing I remember the most from that day was my mom singing "Joseph Smith's First Prayer." To this day, when I hear that song, the emotions come to the surface, and I am transported to a time long ago when my faith was simpler.

After the covenant-making, my grandparents gifted me my first set of scriptures: a white leather set with my name embossed in gold on the cover. Grandma Morine had the most beautiful penmanship and wrote a message inside the front cover.

To our Granddaughter Ganel-Lyn on Baptismal Day 2-16-1979,

This book should be at your side throughout your life as a help and a guide, and if used wisely will help you solve many of life's problems and will be a comfort to you in times of loneliness.

God bless you always,
Grandpa and Grandma Larson

I had no idea forty-four years ago what was in store for that little eight-year-old girl. As my Nana wrote, I have learned over time for myself the truth of her well-developed adult testimony. The scriptures have been a guide and I have kept them by my side, just as Nana counseled. They have helped me solve so many problems and brought comfort during long, lonely nights.

Just because I have had many more life experiences and read many more scriptures, I really don't *know* more today than I did as a newly baptized eight-year-old. I knew then what it felt like to be visited with fire and with the Holy Ghost. Whether it is standing at a pulpit, listening to a cherished Primary song, or studying the scriptures, the Spirit loves responding to our belief.

I remember how happy I felt on that special day. It was a joy that comes when we make and keep covenants. It is the same feeling I felt many years later as I entered the Oakland California Temple as a teenager to do baptisms for the dead. I felt it again at the same temple in 1991 when I received my endowment. I hope and pray that no matter how old I get I never lose the childlike belief and simple faith that leads many of God's eight-year-olds to baptism.

Jesus is our ultimate example. He invites us to follow Him and believe His words. God wants us to have all that He has, an eternal happiness that comes when we make and keep covenants. The Savior taught us in the Sermon on the Mount to heed, believe His words, and be baptized. God wants to give all of us the ultimate gift of salvation and life. His words provides a guide for life. The scriptures give answers to our problems and provide comfort when we are lonely.

POINTS TO PONDER

Do you remember your baptism day? Who was there? Do you remember the music, feelings, or any details?

_____

_____

_____

_____

_____

_____

After Jesus was baptized, the Holy Ghost appeared as a dove. How do you experience the Spirit? Sometimes we make it just about crying, but you may feel it in joy, with music, or through an increase in knowledge. Expanding how you feel the Spirit can increase awareness of how often God is talking to you. Write about a time you felt the Spirit.

_____

_____

_____

_____

_____

_____

3

BLESSED ARE THEY
Who Are Poor in Spirit

Yea, blessed are the poor in spirit
who come unto me, for theirs is
the kingdom of heaven.

—3 NEPHI 12:3

Who are the poor in spirit? I don't think that *poor* here says anything about money in a bank account or the make or model of the car you drive. It is the quality of being totally dependent on God.

As I was researching this beatitude, I was flooded with scriptural accounts and verses to consider. But one of my favorites is about flowers: "Consider the lilies of the field, how they grow; they toil not, neither do they spin" (Matthew 6:28). Flowers are, in essence, poor in spirit. They aren't successful because they hustle, have advanced degrees, or a huge social media following. They are completely dependent on God. They know Who created them and live the full measure of their creation with that spirit of trust. God's creations, as a whole, can teach us much about this next promised blessing in the Beatitudes. The birds, plants, animals, trees, and flowers of the earth are poor when it comes to worldly goods, but theirs truly is already the kingdom of heaven. They grow and exist in a state of peace, knowing

15

that peace comes only when they already have trust that everything they need will be provided.

Poor in spirit is much more than what you do or don't own on the outside. It comes in the way you live life from the inside out. This characteristic comes to life when loving God, with your whole heart, brings peace regardless of the size of your house or the luxurious vacations you don't go on. It is feeling blessed regardless of how many blessings you have or think you should have.

I have known many wealthy people who have also maintained a total state of spiritual reliance on God. They are generous in their stewardships and help build the kingdom with what they have saved and acquired. But for the purpose of this chapter, I would like to focus on the countless examples of those in the scriptures and in our day who live financially in need. They have already found the kingdom of heaven because they are blessed to be poor in spirit. These disciples have a confidence that comes not from wise investments or real estate holdings but from relying on heavenly relationships.

God spoke often in the scriptures about poverty and the responsibility of His disciples to care for the poor:

> The Spirit of the Lord is upon me, because he hath anointed me to preach the gospel to the poor; he hath sent me to heal the brokenhearted, to preach deliverance to the captives, and recovering of sight to the blind, to set at liberty them that are bruised. (Luke 4:18)

The characteristics described in this scriptural mission include the poor, brokenhearted, captives, blind, and those who hurt. This verse in Luke teaches us that those who may be in need may also be more open and willing to receive the gospel. Their humility reminds me of both verses 1 and 2 of the sermon. Because of what they lacked, these people already had a greater ability to heed and believe. Jesus was teaching the Nephites and us today that to be truly poor in spirit means we are in line to receive all that He has in the kingdom of heaven.

I wonder if the invitation to teach among the poor tells us more about what we can learn from this demographic and less about what we can do for them. But what stops us? It is sometimes the distraction of our possessions and perceived power that comes with our earthly stewardships. We know the story of the rich man who came to Jesus and asked what was required to have eternal life. After the Savior counseled him to live the commandments, including honoring his parents and not killing anyone, He said that there was one more thing required:

> Then Jesus beholding him loved him, and said unto him, One thing thou lackest: go thy way, **sell whatsoever thou hast, and give to the poor, and thou shalt have treasure in heaven:** and come, take up the cross, and follow me. (Mark 10:21; emphasis added)

Sell or give away his possessions? That was too much for the rich young man to do. He loved his possessions more than he loved God. As he sadly left Jesus, the Savior taught His disciples this important truth: "how hard is it for them that trust in riches to enter into the kingdom of God! It is easier for a camel to go through the eye of a needle, than for a rich man to enter into the kingdom of God" (Mark 10:24–25). Why is it so hard for those who are not poor in spirit to enter the kingdom of God? And why is it easier for the poor in spirit?

Let's look at another scripture story, found in the New Testament, to find an answer, or at least an example. Jesus was in Jerusalem at the temple while the people were paying their tithing. The rich gave a lot of money to the church. And then a certain woman who had little came to pay her offering:

> And there came a certain poor widow, and she threw in *two mites*, which make a farthing.
>
> For all they did cast in of their abundance; but **she of her want did cast in all that she had,** even all her living. (Mark 12:42, 44, emphasis added)

The widow was obviously poor according to the society of the time; more important is that she demonstrated what it means to be poor in spirit. She gave all that she had. It brings me to tears to think about the faith of this woman, and others just like her, who have given *all they had.*

Jesus witnessed the widow's offering, and today He watches as many others, poor in spirit, act in faith while paying tithing, donating time in a calling, or providing a meal to someone in need. Heaven is sometimes the only witness to our faith-filled offerings. But in God's economy, every mite matters.

*   *   *

I can relate somewhat to Jesus as He watched the widow show up and sacrifice. I too have been blessed to watch on the sidelines when the humble, poor in spirit servants of God quietly go about giving all they have. I've seen them signing up to help a neighbor, dropping off groceries, or donating to a mission account anonymously. Each time I catch someone doing as Jesus would have done if He were there, I feel inspired to look at my own actions. It is then that I check myself and ask the hard, honest questions: *Do I truly have godly confidence? Am I willing to give, as the widow did, all that I have in exchange for a trust that comes in total reliance on Him who wants to give us all? Or do I still sometimes hold back, afraid in scarcity that too much is being asked of me and that somehow heaven's resources will run out?*

My friend Elsie[1] recently had her own modern-day widow's mite story. She was busy caring for five young children and serving as the ward Relief Society president. On top of that, her family was experiencing a painful and prolonged financial struggle.

One afternoon Elsie looked in her refrigerator and realized she had only one pound of ground beef. There was nothing else for dinner. Then she received a worried phone call from the bishop explaining that another family in the ward was in dire need of a meal. Because of the lateness of day, Elsie did not want to try to find another sister to help with the meal. So, she agreed to provide what she could. Little did the bishop know that she would be giving all she had.

---

1. Name has been changed.

Elsie went to her refrigerator and pulled out the lonely pound of ground beef and placed it in the skillet. Her kids, smelling the aroma of dinner, came running, excited to find out what she was cooking for them. Holding back tears, Elsie told her children that the food was for another family. She finished preparations, loaded the meager meal in the car, and drove it to the ward members in need.

As she climbed back into her car, the tears overflowed. She could no longer hold back the worry and fatigue of a mother's heart. What was she going to do? How was she going to feed her own family? Just then her husband, Roger,[2] called. His voice was filled with excitement as he said, "You will not believe what just happened! Brother Smith just called. He just bought and butchered a cow and doesn't have room for half of the meat. He is bringing over half a cow's worth of meat to give us!" Now Elsie was crying tears of gratitude for the tender mercies of God. Brother Smith had no idea that he was part of a mighty miracle for Roger's family.

Faith-promoting stories don't always have a happy ending. The struggle may go on longer than is comfortable while you wait on your miracle cow. But I hope that as you consider Elsie and her faith and willingness to give what she had, that you too will feel the Spirit whisper to you, "Consider the lilies; I see them, and I see that you are giving all that you have." I know you are sometimes afraid, but heaven is near.

Jesus is inviting us to become *poor in spirit* not because a new car or nice vacation is bad but because He knows that when we develop this Christlike attribute, we learn an interdependence with God that opens us up to so much more than what a 401k can provide. As you patiently wait for the windows of heaven to open, trust that you are becoming more like Jesus. "For ye know the grace of our Lord Jesus Christ, that, though he was rich, yet for your sakes he became poor, that ye through his poverty might be rich" (2 Corinthians 8:9). If paying tithing takes the faith Peter had to walk on water, I hope you will be inspired by a certain widow and a certain woman named Elsie, *for theirs* truly *is the kingdom of heaven.*

---

2. Name has been changed.

POINTS TO PONDER

Take a few minutes to consider where you are feeling vulnerable right now. Is it with your health, relationships, finances, or spirituality? Sometimes it is in the places we feel the most anxiety that we struggle to give back from. Can you give from these stewardships (finances, time, service, relationships) and see how God consecrates your offering?

_____

_____

_____

_____

_____

_____

Do you have your own widow's mite or miracle cow story? Write about what happened, how it felt, and the blessings that came from the experience. Consider sharing your faith-promoting experiences with a friend. Power comes in our remembering.

_____

_____

_____

_____

_____

_____

4

BLESSED ARE THEY

Who Mourn

---

*And again, blessed are all they that mourn,
for they shall be comforted.*

—3 NEPHI 12:4

One of the beautiful aspects of the Beatitudes is the gentleness with which the Savior teaches these principles. He is inviting us to grow, develop, and change line upon line, precept upon precept. He isn't demanding perfection today, but is asking each of us to honestly consider the condition of our hearts, our relationships, and our everyday living.

One of my favorite blessings is the one directed to all who are mourning. Jesus promises that they *will be* comforted. I love the assurance given in this verse. He specifically promises those who have lost something or someone that they will not be left alone in their pain. Isn't it beautiful to consider that the blessing is given to those who are bereaved? Christ is making sure we know that no matter how much we are hurting and grieving, He will be there. It feels like God is making sure we don't skip over feeling our feelings.

Because we know about the great plan of happiness and eternal life, we sometimes don't allow ourselves to fully grieve. President

Nelson said: "Irrespective of age, we mourn for those loved and lost. Mourning is one of the deepest expressions of pure love. . . . Moreover, we can't fully appreciate joyful reunions later without tearful separations now. The only way to take sorrow out of death is to take love out of life."[1]

Let's look to Jesus to teach us, by example, when it comes to fully feeling all the feels. Do you remember the story of Mary, Martha, and their brother, Lazarus, who lived in Bethany? Jesus's friends needed him. Lazarus was sick, and his sisters had faith that Jesus could heal him. They sent for Him, but He didn't come in time. Before he even returned to Bethany, Jesus knew that Lazarus had died.

When the Savior arrived, Lazarus had been dead for four days. His sisters were grieving. We read in the book of John, "Then said Martha unto Jesus, Lord, if thou hadst been here, my brother had not died. But I know, that even now, whatsoever thou wilt ask of God, God will give it thee." She expressed faith that even though her brother was genuinely dead, anything is possible with God. "[And] Jesus saith unto her, Thy brother shall rise again" (John 11:21–23).

Jesus taught about the Resurrection and promises that Lazarus would be raised from the dead. But then came one of the most tender, moving, and important scriptures: "Jesus wept" (John 11:35). In one verse we are taught an entire sermon. The Savior knew that Lazarus had been dead for four days and that He would raise Lazarus from the dead. But still Jesus wept. He cried for and with Mary and Martha and their loss. He was their friend, so the loss was deeply personal. His tears reflected the deep love Jesus had for Lazarus. Here was the Son of God, who understood the power to raise someone from the dead, and He chose to experience the feelings instead of skipping over them.

Jesus then went to the tomb and "again groaning in himself cometh to the grave. It was a cave, and a stone lay upon it" (John 11:38). Before calling forth Lazarus from the dead, Jesus wept. If we only know this one aspect of the Savior's character, what changes for us as we navigate our own mortal mourning? Jesus knows how to meet us in our pain. He doesn't hold back, although we sometimes hold back from

---

1. Russell M. Nelson, "Doors of Death," *Ensign* or *Liahona*, May 1992, 72.

weeping and groaning to God. Because Christ experienced all that we will experience, He meets us with His perfect grace and empathy.

* * *

Weeping is an attribute of Christ. Mourning doesn't mean you don't have faith or that you don't believe. It means you have loved and lost. Have you found yourself, like Jesus, groaning and weeping in the wake of loss? Have you tried to sit with those who are mourning in hopes of offering some comfort just as our baptismal covenants ask us to do? That covenant says, "Yea, and are willing to mourn with those that mourn; yea, and comfort those that stand in need of comfort."[2]

I have spoken often about the loss of my forty-year-old sister, Meggan, to suicide. But our family also lost another precious daughter. Just a few months after my beautiful baptism day, on the twelfth of June, my mom gave birth to my baby sister, Bonnie. She was practically perfect in every way—except for the two holes in her heart. She was like a beacon of light in any room she was in. She raised the bar for our family and made us want to be better. Have you ever been in the room with someone so pure in heart that it feels like heaven is near? That was Bonnie.

She had open-heart surgery when she was just a few hours old and spent a few weeks in the newborn intensive care unit (NICU) alongside other babies fighting for their lives. Then we had the gift of having her home for an entire year. I was almost nine years old and Bonnie's self-proclaimed second mommy. I loved taking care of her, feeding her, and dressing her. Bonnie never got strong enough to walk on her own, but she took steps along the side of the couch by holding on to the furniture.

We had some family friends with a baby close to Bonnie's age. Their little boy also had a heart condition. One day we got word that the Clingers' baby had died. He had not done well after his recent surgery, and now his family was swimming in the pool of loss, funeral preparation, and grieving.

---

2. Mosiah 18:9.

I remember very clearly sitting at the Clingers' funeral. It was my first. I can't recall any specifics from the service but have memorized my feelings and something I said in the car after the internment. I told my parents how I felt about the music and how much faith I had that we would not ever have to have a funeral for Bonnie. I boldly declared my eight-year-old faith in the power of prayer and priesthood blessings that my family had received. The Clingers' funeral had been sad but peaceful.

I remember my parents specifically reaching out to the Clinger family and a number of other NICU families who were grieving. My parents were teaching me by example what it looked like to help others even when you need help yourself. They have always been good at that. Even though they had doctor appointments, a sick little baby, and two other little girls who needed their support and attention, I remember my mom on the phone with other mothers and taking meals to families that had babies still in the hospital.

When Bonnie was a year old, the doctors wanted to try to permanently correct her heart defect in the hope of extending her life. The surgery went well, and everyone was hopeful. But then Bonnie slipped into a coma. Her heart seemed to be better, but her body was too weak to handle the surgery. Other systems were shutting down. Bonnie was in a coma in the NICU for more than a month. I still had faith that our outcome would be different than that of our friends' baby. Then on July 25, 1980, Bonnie passed away. Her little body could no longer hold on.

Her funeral was a powerful missionary moment. Two pews were filled with doctors and nurses who had cared for Bonnie. My mom had copies of the Book of Mormon embossed with their names as gifts for their devotion. It felt like hundreds of friends and loved ones came to mourn with our family. I remember looking at Bonnie's sweet, little, peaceful face in the casket, where we had placed some of her favorite toys to be buried with her. We stood and hugged and cried and talked with mourners.

I remember distinctly the Clingers coming to support us in our time of need. We had mourned with them, and now they, in empathy and understanding, were mourning with us. There were so many flowers, meals, and phone calls coming into our home. Months before, I had witnessed flowers, meals, and phone calls going out of our home to others.

Our family is anxiously anticipating the day when we will be reunited with both of my beautiful sisters and many others who have gone on before us. I recently saw a post that showed the size of grief. Over time, our grief doesn't get smaller, but our capacity to hold the grief grows bigger. I saw the capacity grow in the Clingers and in my own family. Losing someone expands our ability to mourn with those that mourn. Then, like Jesus, when we weep, we find beautiful new ways to reach others in their weeping. Maybe the promised blessing in this beatitude comes because we are comforted when we provide comfort. We are never truly alone in our mourning when we keep our baptismal covenants to mourn with those that mourn.

POINTS TO PONDER

Take a moment and journal about feelings of loss, sadness, and grief. Maybe it isn't connected with the loss of a person but a loss of health, a job, or a friendship. Don't skip over the weeping.

_____

_____

_____

_____

_____

_____

_____

Who do you know that is mourning? What can you do to help that person? Consider a time in your life when you were supported in your grief. How did people show up for you? What helped? What didn't? How can you give back and mourn with those that mourn this week?

_____

_____

_____

_____

_____

_____

_____

_____

_____

_____

_____

_____

5

BLESSED ARE THEY

Who Are Meek

Blessed are the meek,
for they shall inherit the earth.

—3 NEPHI 12:5

How are you doing with your study of the words and teachings of Jesus? Are you starting to feel a greater connection with the Savior? If there were only thirteen verses of scriptures for you to read and internalize, I hope this featured collection is filling you with joy, hope, and love. But we are only about halfway through the sermon.

One of the most powerful and possibly underappreciated characteristics of Christ is *meekness*. Consider the Savior of the world, the Creator of universes, teaching of the importance of meekness.

> I cannot comprehend his power, his majesty, his perfections. But I do understand something of his love, his compassion, his mercy. There is no burden he cannot lift. There is no heart he cannot purify and fill with joy. There is no life he cannot cleanse and restore when one is obedient to his teachings.[1]

---

1. Richard G. Scott, "True Friends That Lift," *Ensign* or *Liahona*, November 1988, 77.

How poignant it is to ponder on the potential we each have to inherit the earth. Here in His sermon, Jesus helps us open up the ultimate eternal investment account. The only deposit we need to make is our meekness. God is asking us to willingly give up our pride, and in return He will give us the entire earth.

Jesus said, "Take my yoke upon you, and learn of me; for I am meek and lowly in heart: and ye shall find rest unto your souls" (Matthew 11:29). My *Talk of Him* co-host, John Fossum, loved to invite our viewers *to get yoked*. Just like the heavy lifting done at gyms around the world, the weight of mortality can be oppressive at times. But when we yoke ourselves with the Savior, He can make the unbearable bearable. He is the ultimate lifting partner, spotting, assisting, and cheering you on when you are weary and wobbly. As we yoke ourselves with Jesus, His strengths become ours. The Savior is telling us that if we partner with Him, we must learn of Him. And then Jesus promises His meek and lowly heart, where you will find rest.

I find it intriguing and inspiring to consider that as we *get yoked* with Jesus, His meekness and heart provide a much-needed rest. Some are called to lift a life of worldly weights. Addiction, anxiety, arthritis, and Alzheimer's disease are just the beginning of the lifetime of lifting some are called to manage. God isn't asking us to do any spiritual, emotional, mental, or physical lifting alone. Your capacity is expanded through the grace and meekness of Jesus. Meekness is not weakness. Jesus is teaching us by example. When the world says blessings come only when you hustle and haggle more, heaven teaches to simply try humility.

* * *

Who do you think about when I say *meek*? What faces and names come to your mind? Do you have a neighbor who always quietly pulls the garbage cans up to the house or shovels the widow's walkway? Or how about the gentle lunch lady who secretly sneaks an extra scoop of chocolate pudding on the tray of a struggling second-grader surviving his parents' divorce? There are countless examples of the meek and humble, people who have really brought scriptures to life with how they live and love.

As I prayed about who to write about, the first name that came to my heart was Lauren. Anyone who knew her knows exactly why she's the perfect example of meekness. I met Lauren during her senior year of high school. She started attending our daughter's weekly Preach My Gospel discussion held in our basement every Sunday. My son started PMG when he was sixteen, and over the years it has grown. The names and faces have changed, but the same beautiful spirit comes into our home every week when a variety of teens, young single adults, full-time missionaries, and married couples come to talk about the gospel. It isn't our calling, but we love hosting authentic and vulnerable conversations about addiction, anxiety, and the Atonement of Christ.

My daughter and Lauren attended the same school and had mutual friends. Lauren was a gifted athlete and was kind to everyone she met. She came to PMG every week, although at first, she rarely said much. Our basement was like a sardine can as we squeezed as many as sixty believers and sometimes nonbelievers in the house at one time. I loved being Momma Condie to these kids and hugging them every week.

Lauren had experienced some big life challenges with the death of her father when she was very young. She had also suffered a number of sports injuries that led to multiple surgeries. When she started coming to our group, Lauren had just had another knee surgery and was in a leg brace. Because of that, she sat on the stairs with me and my husband, Rob, instead of on the floor or couch with the other PMG kids. Over the weeks, we talked with Lauren, learned more about her family, and felt of her gentle spirit. She made a number of comments that changed me. But what inspired me most about Lauren was witnessing her willingness to be meek. I never heard her complain about all the setbacks and heartbreaks. Instead, she meekly made her way through physical therapy and senior prom.

Because of all the injuries, Lauren wasn't sure she would ever be able to play collegiate sports. But God promises that those who are meek will eventually inherit the earth, and that happened to Lauren before high school graduation. She had rehabilitated her knee enough to play on the women's soccer team at Eastern Utah University. She was ecstatic.

Graduation came and went, and we continued to meet in our basement. Some of our PMG kids were getting mission calls and leaving for school in other parts of the world. Fall came, and PMG was now happening only monthly. My daughter, Brooklyn, came home from BYU on the weekends. It was awesome to see some of the PMGers who lived close by and could still come.

I remember one of the last times we saw Lauren. It was in the fall after school had started, and Lauren surprised us all by coming to PMG. She shared with us her recent desire to serve a mission as soon as possible. She had previously decided to postpone serving a mission so she could play a couple of seasons of soccer first. Lauren had worked hard to do physical therapy and train so she could keep playing. But now, even though she was enjoying college, she felt an urgency to go on a mission as soon as possible. Lauren was reading conference talks, studying her scriptures, playing soccer, and was happier than ever.

Then one rainy October evening, while driving back to college, she hydroplaned, spinning into an oncoming truck. Lauren was killed. Her family and friends, teachers, and teammates were in shock and grieving. Our hearts were broken. Lauren's light was so bright.

As we stood in the long line of mourners at her viewing, we looked at a lifetime of pictures, trophies, and memories. One of Lauren's prized possessions was her *Preach My Gospel* manual. Her mom, Vera Lyn, shared with us how much Lauren had loved and appreciated coming to our home to talk about faith and feelings.

Now we knew why Lauren had felt such an urgency to serve a mission. She *was* being called to serve a mission—just much sooner than any of us thought. Lauren is now teaching and helping in a different capacity than any of us had imagined. Many of her friends are already in the mission field. Some are waiting to put on their black badges and formally knock on doors. But all who knew and loved Lauren, especially those doing missionary work on this side of the veil, are and will be serving with a greater purpose and focus.

My daughter, Brooklyn, said it perfectly the Sunday morning we got word of Lauren's accident: "I am more certain of *my* why for serving a mission than I was two days ago. I am going to share Jesus with those who don't know Him. I am going to share the gospel with those who have lost people they love and don't know about eternal life."

In the wake of Lauren's death, many of her friends and loved ones have had to work through big feelings of sadness, loss, and grief. Because of the plan of happiness, we know we will be together again. Until that day, we can keep the memories of Lauren alive by how we live our lives. One of the characteristics people admired the most about Lauren was her meek and kind heart. Everyone who knew her loved her. And in many ways, Lauren's example and influence is still being spread around the world as her friends go out into the mission field to share the gospel and teach of Christ.

I am so grateful and honored for the time we were blessed to see meekness in action in the life of dear Lauren. The world may not usually celebrate meekness, but when the world loses the influence of the meek, as in the case of Lauren, the world deeply feels their absence.

POINTS TO PONDER

Who are the people you know who most effectively emulate meekness? Consider sending them a text, card, or voice message honoring their example and influence on you.

_____

_____

_____

_____

_____

_____

_____

What stops you from showing up in meekness? Is it fear, comparison, or anxiety? Journal about places and situations you can share meekness and how it can help improve an outcome.

_____

_____

_____

_____

_____

_____

_____

_____

6

BLESSED ARE THEY

Who Hunger and Thirst after Righteousness

And blessed are all they who do hunger
and thirst after righteousness, for they shall
be filled with the Holy Ghost.

—3 NEPHI 12:6

Have you ever been so hungry and thirsty that all you could think about was food and water? This kind of focus creates an energy that propels someone to search high and low and to savor what they discover when they finally find what they are looking for. Do we have this same kind of appetite for righteousness? We are living in a world that preaches "everything goes" and "you do you." "Eat, drink, and be merry, for tomorrow is tomorrow!" Hungering after righteousness is rarely celebrated.

Look at what Jesus is teaching in the verse above. He is inviting His followers to desire righteousness, and if they do, He promises that they will be filled and blessed by the Holy Ghost. Our access to God's power increases as we make and keep covenants. There are so many distractions in the world—instant gratification, following after fun, and doing what makes you happy seem to be the mottoes of mortality. But God is always inviting us to a higher and holier way. We learn that real right is not relative.

Let's turn to the scriptures for more inspiration and understanding about what it may look like to hunger and thirst after righteousness. One of my favorite scripture heroines is Deborah, an Israeli prophetess. While the Canaanites ruled over the Israelites, the Israelites stopped keeping the commandments. It took twenty years for the Israelites to humble themselves and ask the Lord for help.

After gathering an army, Barak was called to be Israel's military leader. He was afraid but said that if Deborah was by his side, he would not fear. Deborah agreed to help the army and prophesied that a woman would defeat the Canaanite army's leader. Deborah and Barak came down from the mountain and rallied the soldiers to trust the Lord. She was filled with the Spirit and testified in a way that fortified the faith of her people. After a rainstorm washed away a majority of the Canaanite army, a woman appeared, just as Deborah prophesied, and defeated Sisera, the enemy's military leader (see Judges 4).

Remembering can be one of the biggest tools in our conversion toolboxes. Deborah knew about the power of righteousness and *remembering*. She sang a song so that Israel would never forget what the Lord did for them. The Israelites lived peacefully for the next forty years. Because they kept the commandments (see Judges 5), Deborah protected her people in *her* righteousness. She demonstrated to Barak a steadiness and godly confidence that only comes as fruit of the Spirit. She stood steadfast with the Spirit when the storm was surging.

What can we learn from this military story? Life is a battle. And the enemy wants us to rely on the arm of the flesh. But as the book of Judges demonstrates, nothing is too big for our God. When we trust in truth and right, we can walk onto our personal battlefields with confidence in our covenants and a relationship with God.

* * *

I am blessed to know many modern-day Deborahs. They are women of great faith who strengthen me to face my own fears and inspire me to stay steadfast in the storms. As faith friends, we regularly discuss our personal holy habits such as scripture study, meditation, temple attendance, and prayer. We fast together and pray for each other. Just like Barak did with Deborah, I have turned to these *certain women* when my faith feels wobbly.

Each of my Deborahs has her own set of specific spiritual gifts. My dear friend Shawna receives personal revelation in dreams. Andrea is gifted with meditation. Sunny fosters righteousness in serving so many in her family and community. Amy has taught me more about where God's power is found in His creations. Jenny and Ari are in tune with the Spirit and help me turn up the volume when heaven is quiet and my self-doubt is screaming.

Rhonna has taught me so much about the power of speaking in faith and our connection with family history. She committed to doing temple work or genealogy every day for an entire year. One day I was struggling to write a really important talk that would be heard by tens of thousands of people. Still recovering from a wrist accident and not having full mobility in my hand, I was weighed down with worry about finishing this book, my children's needs, and other commitments. I felt empty. I was tired and doubting that I could even hear the voice of the Spirit to be inspired.

I prayed, pondered, and petitioned heaven for help. And then the prompting came to text my faith friend Rhonna. I wrote: "I am asking for prayers and help with some big writing projects. I feel like heaven is silent."

Within moments, Rhonna responded to my message with a personal and powerful prayer. The words were both bold and beautiful. Here is a portion of what she shared with me: "Remember: this is His work and you are giving glory to Him with your eye single to Jesus! You are filled with His light. With Christ you are fully equipped to create and speak the word to witness of Christ. The Light of Christ will flood your mind, body and spirit. And you are connected to heaven to know of a surety what God wants you to speak."

That digital prayer was what I needed to face the enemy of doubt and fear that was flooding my head. I loved that Rhonna had done the daily work needed to be in a position to witness to me. The truth wasn't about my limitations but that this was God's work, and the glory always goes to Him.

I started to write. Slowly and steadily, the words started to flow and so did my tears. I was crying because I could feel the Spirit clearly with me in my home office. I could hear the words come into my heart and mind. Heaven had been far away just moments earlier, but now it was close. In answer to Rhonna's prayer, I felt my mind, body, and spirit fill with faith and light.

It truly is in the small daily choices that we fill our wells of faith. When we use our agency to seek after truth and right, with just one verse of scripture and daily prayer, the water will be there when we are thirsty and need to draw from it. So, when you get spiritually dehydrated and malnourished, keep reaching and hungering. And look to your faithful friends! Especially when you don't know where to go for that heavenly hydration and divine delectables. Your faith friends can help. They don't have to be your best friends. But find people who have faced their own battles, wrestled in war, and clung to their covenants. And don't do it alone.

I am blessed to have Deborahs march alongside me on earth. They daily hunger, seek, and thirst after righteousness. They live with the companionship of the Spirit. Be willing to be vulnerable. Barak confessed to Deborah that he was afraid. It was then that she stepped up and showed him and her people the power that comes when someone is willing to nourish a relationship with God and trust Him above all else.

POINTS TO PONDER

What are your daily holy habits where you hunger and thirst after righteousness?

_____

_____

_____

_____

_____

_____

_____

_____

_____

_____

There is power in remembering. Can you remember a time when you faced an enemy with godly confidence? What happened? How did you feel the Holy Ghost inspire and direct you?

_____

_____

_____

_____

_____

_____

_____

7

BLESSED ARE THEY
Who Are Merciful

And blessed are the merciful,
for they shall obtain mercy.

—3 NEPHI 12:7

The author C. S. Lewis said it best: "To be a Christian means to forgive the inexcusable because God has forgiven the inexcusable in you."[1] If you want to be Christian, try to be like Christ. I don't know if there is a better definition about why the Beatitudes matter. These teachings are so much about Jesus sitting with His followers, inviting them into His world, sharing His view and way of living and loving. I hope you are beginning to visualize what it will be like to someday sit at the Savior's feet and gaze up at His face. What will you be feeling? Are you squirming in your seat, anxious about being enough or measuring up? I hope that when you think about sitting with Christ, you feel only love.

He is not frustrated with you. He is not disappointed in you. He has been and will always be cheering you on, for eternity. God is constantly inviting you to walk with Him and become happier because

---

1. www.goodreads.com

you are becoming more like Him. Don't get discouraged. You are following a merciful Teacher. As Elder Holland stated, "Surely the thing God enjoys most about being God is the thrill of being merciful, especially to those who don't expect it and often feel they don't deserve it."[2] Don't give up.

I have a confession: as a recovering perfectionist, the principle of mercy is a constant work in progress for me. Often we struggle with *giving* mercy because we struggle with *receiving* mercy. In other words, we can give only what we have to give. We can't give a gift we don't have to give. I love studying, researching, and learning more about examples of mercy from the scriptures. There are so many. Just look under the topical guide and you will be filled and inspired.

In the days leading up to His Crucifixion, Christ was betrayed by His closest friends, was mocked by onlookers, healed the ear of a Roman soldier, and was crowned with thorns:

And the people stood beholding. And the rulers also with them derided him, saying, He saved others; let him save himself, if he be Christ, the chosen of God.

And the soldiers also mocked him, coming to him, and offering him vinegar,

And saying, If thou be the king of the Jews, save thyself.

And a superscription also was written over him in letters of Greek, and Latin, and Hebrew, THIS IS THE KING OF THE JEWS. (Luke 23:35–38)

Whole volumes could be written about the example of forgiveness and mercy Jesus demonstrated in just His last few days of mortality. For the purpose of our study of this beatitude, I want to highlight one of the most powerful moments in scripture—the moment Jesus hung on the cross between two thieves. The soldiers seemed to find pleasure in torturing the Savior of the World. Jesus hung in excruciating pain as His hands and feet were nailed to the cross, the weight of His body crushing the organs inside.

---

2. Holland, "The Laborers in the Vineyard," 33.

For most of us, experiencing such gruesome agony would bring out the worst of our character. But not Jesus. In that moment, when the worst of humanity had been on display, the Savior spoke these merciful words of the soldiers who were killing Him: "Father, *forgive them; for they know not what they do.* And they parted his raiment, and cast lots" (Luke 23:34; emphasis added).

They know not what they do. What a powerful teaching. Jesus knew the hearts and minds of His murderers. And He said that they didn't know what they were doing. What changes for every one of us when we know the hearts and minds of those who use, abuse, or accuse us? How much easier will it be to forgive when we clearly see each other? And when we clearly see God?

The invitation to be merciful isn't for someday in another time and place. It is a blessing offered to each of us. If we accept it, we will have mercy to give away. The Savior teaches in verse 7 that when we are merciful, we will obtain mercy. We treat people the way we feel about ourselves. Hurt people hurt people. And loved people love people.

It is much easier to write about mercy and forgiveness than it is to live the principle. Many of God's children have survived great trauma and betrayal. How could God ask us to give mercy to those who violate, torture, and abandon the helpless? Isn't God a god of justice as well as mercy? As Jesus invites the gathered crowd to be baptized, to mourn, to be meek, and to hunger, He isn't asking them—and by extension, us—to do this on our own.

He isn't setting the bar high and then telling us to practice jumping. When God invites us to do anything, follow any commandment, or live any principle, He is always extending His grace to enable us to accomplish what is asked of us. Don't rely on the arm of the flesh to be more understanding of your grouchy neighbor, forgive a dishonest business partner, or extend mercy to an addicted sibling. Turn to God to become like Him. Seek His mercy and grace so that you have mercy and grace to give away.

* * *

As I considered the many modern stories of mercy, my heart turned to the many mothers who are working, wrestling, and worrying about their families. One mother, above all, came to my mind. Lisa[3] struggled with immense mental health issues. As a single mom, she worked full-time to support her two children. She would often find herself pushed to anger and depression. Although she deeply loved her kids, she struggled to love herself. Lisa wanted to be more patient but wasn't able to be patient with herself. But she kept trying.

Her oldest child, Michelle,[4] watched and wondered what more she could do to help her mommy feel happier and help keep her younger brother, Mathew, safe. There were road trips and dance parties, but underneath the happiness were some big wells of sadness. Then one day Lisa met a kind man and they fell in love. They married and eventually had more children of their own. With this new marriage and children there was more love. But with each new baby, Lisa's mental health became ever more strained.

It was not unusual for Lisa's depression and anger to reach violent levels. She frequently felt suicidal and made multiple attempts to end her life. During these emotional episodes, Michelle was commonly left in charge at home with her younger siblings, panicked and afraid. She understandably feared what would happen to her mom.

Lisa was one of the most giving women in her community. She volunteered to help anyone in need, served in multiple church callings, and worked very hard to provide her family with all they needed. But she rarely seemed happy. What Lisa's children came to eventually understand about their mother was that Lisa's own mother had left her when she was very young. Her father had struggled to provide a safe and steady home for Lisa. She was now trying to mother without an example of mothering. The combination of Lisa's childhood trauma, mental health needs, and the demands of a young family had pushed her to a habitually dark and anxious place.

Lisa was impatient with her kids but was more impatient with herself. It was easier for Lisa to forgive others for their imperfections than to receive forgiveness for her own. But Lisa never stopped trying to get help and answers. She consistently met with therapists and medical

---

3. Name has been changed.
4. Name has been changed.

doctors and reached out to supportive friends. Daily reality took its toll on everyone.

As the oldest in the home, Michelle worked hard at school with a goal of leaving home and going to college. She dreamed and prayed that someday she could break the cycles of anger and abuse from her childhood. She wanted to keep the faith and spirit of service she had witnessed, but she definitely wanted to do things differently.

After leaving home and starting school, Michelle started meeting with a therapist. It was there that she began to understand more about how her childhood had led to some extreme perfectionism. It had been a protection. She mistakenly believed that if she was perfect, maybe she could control and stop something bad from happening to her or someone she loved. Michelle knew that her mother, Lisa, had done the very best she could. Michelle learned that in order to have a healthy relationship with her mother, boundaries were necessary.

Michelle eventually married a wonderful man that had come from a very different background where yelling was rare. No one had been divorced. Eventually, they became parents. Sitting alone with her little baby girl in their small apartment, Michelle cried and prayed for heaven's help. Her husband had gone back to work, and she felt overwhelmed with the responsibility now sleeping in her arms. There was so much to do as a mom, from feeding schedules, homework, dentist appointments, FHE lessons, and maybe a mission. How could she raise this precious child the way God wanted? How could she create a safe home where her child would be able to develop in healthy ways? How could she do things better?

Michelle had read all the parenting books. She had asked her baby's pediatrician all her questions. Michelle was now responsible for raising another human. Astounded at her baby's little fingers and toes, she recognized a deep and sincere new love like she had never experienced before. This love wasn't just for her baby, but also a profound sense of gratitude and mercy for her own parents. Michelle felt a new appreciation and understanding for her mother. Yes, Lisa had made many mistakes, but she had also given Michelle the spirit of generosity and the gospel. Lisa had shown her children loyalty and love in the only way she knew how.

Over the years, people have asked Michelle how she could maintain a loving relationship with her mother. The answer was simple. Lisa had always taken responsibility for her mistakes. This had made it easier to extend mercy. The truth is that the moment someone becomes a parent, it becomes clear that God has never created perfect parents. Every child will deal with the flaws of family life. Babies grow up to have babies of their own, and the cycle continues. Michelle, like so many other children in the world from similar circumstances, saw the heart of her mother more clearly when she herself became a mother.

I don't think anyone becomes a parent and plans to mess up. No mother I know is lying awake at night thinking of ways to make life harder for their children. But the truth is that we keep messing up. All of us. Michelle and Lisa have continued over the years to forgive one another. They have both learned how to manage motherhood in healthier ways and extend mercy to themselves as quickly as they extend it to others. It hasn't been easy. At times both women have struggled to face old pain and find a new way forward. But through Christ, all things are possible. Even the hard things.

I love what Sister Kristin Yee vulnerably shared in the October 2022 general conference about the difficult relationship she once had with her earthly father:

> As my love for the Savior has grown, so has my desire to replace hurt and anger with His healing balm. It has been a process of many years, requiring courage, vulnerability, perseverance, and learning to trust in the Savior's divine power to save and heal. I still have work to do, but my heart is no longer on a warpath. I have been given "a new heart"—one that has felt the deep and abiding love of a personal Savior, who stayed beside me, who gently and patiently led me to a better place, who wept with me, who knew my sorrow.[5]

---

5. Kristin Yee, "Beauty for Ashes: The Healing Path of Forgiveness," *Liahona*, November 2022, 37.

In the same address, Sister Yee shares that her father has had a change of heart, something she never thought was possible in this life. I know finding these happy endings aren't always how mortality plays out for those who also go to God, fast, pray, get therapy, and keep trying. But healing is possible. Even if it may not be until the next life.

Elder Richard G. Scott taught: "You cannot erase what has been done, but you can forgive. Forgiveness heals terrible, tragic wounds, for it allows the love of God to purge your heart and mind of the poison of hate. . . . It makes place for the purifying, healing, restoring love of the Lord."[6]

It is a process. But it is worth all our effort. We can each do a little more each day to not only seek for but also receive the gift of Christ's mercy. For blessed are the merciful because they will truly receive mercy. We cannot give what we don't receive. So, if your scars and sins are severe, accept this invitation of more mercy from the Savior.

POINTS TO PONDER

Who has really hurt you? Maybe it is someone to whom you haven't been able to fully extend mercy. Consider writing a letter to that person. Express all the feelings, hurts, and memories. You don't have to send this letter.

_____

_____

_____

_____

_____

_____

6. Richard G. Scott, "Healing the Tragic Scars of Abuse," *Ensign* or *Liahona*, May 1992, 33.

Now take the letter you have written and share it with God. Talk to Him about how you really feel. Take the letter you wrote and consider burning it or ripping it up. Are you now better able to ask for mercy for yourself and for the person who hurt you?

_____

_____

_____

_____

_____

_____

_____

8

BLESSED ARE THEY

Who Are Pure in Heart

And blessed are all the pure in heart,
for they shall see God.

—3 NEPHI 12:8

Over the last thirty years, I have lived with a serious heart condition connected with my lupus diagnosis. It is interesting to have something that can be life-threatening and painful but felt only on the inside without being seen on the outside. To everyone else, I look absolutely fine, while I am hurting so much inside. My cardiologist can see what condition my heart is in by reading reports and ordering tests. I can feel my heart hurting and know when it is doing better. But even then, I am not always sure of its specific state of physical wellness. It is the same with the spiritual and emotional state of our hearts. God is the ultimate cardiologist. He is aware of how your heart is doing.

Jesus teaches the next beatitude about the purity of our hearts with one of the most beautiful of all the blessings: those who are pure in heart will see God. What more could we hope for, pray for, and work for than this? But how does someone know if a heart is pure?

I use pain and energy levels as signals about how my heart is doing. What signs do we have to assess the purity of a heart?

Consider some of the outward characteristics of an inward condition. The pure in heart exhibit qualities closely connected to other Christlike attributes. Characteristics of kindness, gratitude, and the ability to see the beauty in others signal a heart condition—a grateful heart. For the purpose of our study and personal application of the Beatitudes, let's explore the scriptures for examples of people who lived with kind and grateful hearts. It will likely reveal the pure in heart as well.

During Christ's time, leprosy was frequently mentioned. This disease was more common in ancient times than it is today, but it does still exist. A skin disease that also affected other parts of the body, leprosy caused pain, physical disfiguration, and death. It was considered highly contagious. During the time of Jesus, people with leprosy were forced to live away from the rest of society and were labeled unclean.

Read the miraculous story when Jesus meets and heals ten lepers:

> And it came to pass, as he went to Jerusalem, that he passed through the midst of Samaria and Galilee.
>
> And as he entered into a certain village, there met him ten men that were lepers, which stood afar off:
>
> And they lifted up their voices, and said, Jesus, Master, have mercy on us.
>
> And when he saw them, he said unto them, Go shew yourselves unto the priests. And it came to pass, that, as they went, *they were cleansed*. (Luke 17:11–14; emphasis added)

I love reflecting that their cleansing came *as they went*. The lepers were healed as they moved forward to go show the priests. Think about what actions we must take to receive Christ's healing for ourselves. These men had lived a life of pain and isolation. Maybe they ran to, or skipped to, the religious leaders to finally have the approval and access they had been so wanting. But only one appeared to be truly changed by his encounter with the Savior:

> And one of them, when he saw that he was healed, turned back, and with a loud voice glorified God,

And fell down on his face at his feet, giving him thanks: and he was a Samaritan.

And Jesus answering said, were there not ten cleansed? but where are the nine?

There are not found that returned to give glory to God, save this stranger.

And he said unto him, Arise, go thy way: *thy faith hath made thee whole.* (Luke 17:15–19; emphasis added)

One out of the ten turned back to thank Jesus. He didn't just quietly express appreciation, but declared with a loud voice, "Glory to God." He fell down on Jesus's feet to thank God for this gift. After this intimate moment of communion, the Savior instructed the man to stand up and go tell the priests. Ponder the Savior's words: "Thy faith hath made thee whole." Is it possible that the other nine men received a portion of healing but the one who had expressed true appreciation for the gift given was actually made whole?

We can gain even more understanding, in the seventeenth chapter of Luke, about the blessing given to the pure in heart. Is it possible that this one thankful leper not only healed but was made whole because he actually saw God in this miracle? His pure heart is evident from an external expression—that of gratitude—signaling an inner genuine heart condition. President Nelson said:

Over my nine and a half decades of life, I have concluded that counting our blessings is far better than recounting our problems. No matter our situation, showing gratitude for our privileges is a fast-acting and long-lasting spiritual prescription. Does gratitude spare us from sorrow, sadness, grief, and pain? No, but it does soothe our feelings. It provides us with a greater perspective on the very purpose and joy of life.[1]

One in ten had the eyes and heart to truly see. Do we?

---

1. Russell M. Nelson, quoted in "Luke 17:11–19," *New Testament Seminary Teacher Manual* (2023).

* * *

I am excited to introduce you to the epitome of a pure heart. She is the teenage daughter of my *Talk of Him* co-host, John Fossum. Viewers of our show heard John share on the show many personal lessons learned and gifts received from parenting such an extraordinary girl.

I personally have been changed for the better by my association with Rachel and the Fossum family. From our first meeting, I felt like I was in the presence of a visitor from another land. Rachel is easy to love and loves easily. I am a hugger, and I am grateful that Rachel is always willing and eager to share a hug with me. You can't help but feel better after just being in the room with Rachel. She often came into the room while John and I were prepping online for an upcoming taping of *Talk of Him*. She is nonverbal but has a powerful way of clearly communicating her feelings of joy, gratitude, and love. Rachel is a clear example to me of what it means to be pure in heart.

I asked her father, John, to share how he has witnessed his daughter's untainted soul:

> What really stands out to me is how much she loves herself. Like genuinely and humbly loves herself. Just the way she is. When she looks in the mirror, all she sees is beauty. Her teeth are crooked, and she sometimes has horrid teen acne, but she doesn't see it. All she sees is her beauty. She still has awareness about the type of hairstyle she wants and clothes she wears, but she seems to be 100 percent satisfied and joyful about how she looks and who she is. She has perfectly innocent love for herself. The joy and purity that emanate from her because of that love are palpable. She extends the same grace to everyone. She doesn't see "ugly." All she sees is beauty in everyone, including herself. Most of us can see beauty in others, but we choose to see "ugly" too. And most of us struggle with seeing ourselves as ugly or being discontent with who we are. But not Rachel!

What would change in the world if we lived more like Rachel? How would hearts and homes be healed if we only saw beauty in ourselves and others? Even though Rachel lives with obvious limitations when it comes to language and learning, she doesn't seem to be limited in loving. I can't think of a better paragon of purity than in the ability to love ourselves and by extension love others more.

I have seen Rachel express extreme joy and gratitude just for the chance to sing, or a trip to the movies and a special after-school treat. When you see the world as Rachel does, everything is more—more glittery, more magical, more enjoyable. Rachel and the one leper can teach the world about what it truly means to be pure in heart because of how they respond to what they have been given. They both seem to see what others overlook. And they have the ability to ignore the markings and misgivings by which many mortals are myopically sidetracked.

Victor Hugo was right when he penned, "To love another person is to see the face of God."[2] Or in the words of the Sermon on the Mount, to appreciate and love another person you *will see* the face of God.

POINTS TO PONDER

What is the difference between being healed of leprosy and being made whole? Have you experienced healing and wholeness? Journal about how you may have received both.

_____

_____

_____

_____

_____

_____

_____

---

2. www. goodreads.com

Have a gratitude prayer today. Don't ask for anything; instead frame everything in your prayer as an expression of thanks. How does praying with this attitude of gratitude change the spirit of your prayer?

_____

_____

_____

_____

_____

_____

_____

_____

9

BLESSED ARE THEY

Who Are Peacemakers

And blessed are all the peacemakers,
for they shall be called the children of God.

—3 NEPHI 12:9

As we investigate and experiment on the final two beatitudes, I hope your heart has already begun to feel different. I was trying to review what has felt different about this writing project from my previous publications. Then it became clear. My singular focus for this book has been to share the words and teachings of Jesus. His teachings have inspired other great thought leaders, such as C. S. Lewis and Elder Holland, to expand and apply these Christlike principles in our modern life. And in the process, hopefully you have been motivated as well. Because the nucleus of these words has been Him, God has felt even closer in the process. My prayer has been that even if the circumstances of your life may not have changed, Jesus has changed your perspective for the better.

As we study these words and verses, the volume of God's voice is turned up. We don't need to feel alone or permanently anxious when using our agency to access the Atonement of Christ. Jesus is inviting all to come and sit with Him, learn of Him, and walk in His footsteps.

As we do this, we begin to feel a greater companionship with the Spirit, and as a result of your review of this sacred text, you are blessed with His comfort, mercy, and spirit.

In a world where daily headlines scream of war and heartbreak, peace becomes a precious and priceless possession. But where can you find this peace? God invites His children in 3 Nephi 12:9 to be the source of peace by becoming a peacemaker. I anticipate that when we meet the Savior face to face, we will first feel love; then we will feel immense peace. Jesus is known by many names, but one that is needed most today is peace. "For He is our peace" (Ephesians 2:14).

When Jesus lived among the Apostles, He went about healing, teaching, and giving. His ministry was a mission of peace. We read in the book of Mark, chapter four, about Jesus and His disciples in a boat. After a long day, the Savior was asleep. But as they journeyed upon the water, a great storm arose. The waves grew in intensity, as well as the anxiety of the Apostles, so they woke up Jesus.

> And he was in the hinder part of the ship, asleep on a pillow: and they awake him, and say unto him, Master, carest thou not that we perish?
>
> And he arose, and rebuked the wind, and said unto the sea, Peace, be still. And the wind ceased, and there was a great calm.
>
> And he said unto them, Why are ye so fearful? how is it that ye have no faith?
>
> And they feared exceedingly, and said one to another, What manner of man is this, that even the wind and the sea obey him? (Mark 4:38–41)

Just as Jesus calmed the raging seas, He can calm our raging hearts. When fear takes over and threatens to destroy and overtake our faith, we can do as the Apostles did and turn to the Savior, for He is the ultimate source of peace. And through Him, as we take upon ourselves His name, we can share that peace with a war-ravaged world. If you are afraid that He doesn't care about the storms of your soul, trust that God sees you and knows your circumstances. He does not sleep when you are troubled. Wake up your reliance on the Prince of Peace. Even the wind and the sea obey His commands.

* * *

One of my fondest desires was to have a home and family culture where peace rules. My daily efforts and prayers as a mother seemed to solely focus on providing a place of peace where my children could grow and make mistakes. I wanted them to feel confident that they were always safe both emotionally and physically.

From the moment we brought little—or not-so-little—ten-pound baby Cameron home from the hospital, Rob and I worked hard to practice patience, repent regularly, and forgive frequently. It wasn't always easy, and we were definitely not perfect parents. But we decided that peace was a priority.

We were over the moon when in early January 2004, our dear daughter, Brooklyn, was born. It was obvious from the first moment the doctors handed her to me that she brought with her a powerful spirit. I know every mom says that about their babies, but I was struck almost immediately with a feeling of peace when I held her. In many ways, her spirit reminded me so much of my late sister Bonnie.

As Brooklyn grew, the magic we felt in our home was shared with her friends, classmates, and theater directors. When we struggled to make a family decision, choose a movie, or try to fairly play a board game, it was frequently Brooklyn who would step up and step in as the peacemaker.

Even though I committed to always having love and kindness in our home, I often fell short. There were still times of conflict and contention. And when those normal family storms surfaced, I sometimes panicked, fearing that my children had been seriously hurt or damaged because of a stressful skirmish. It was often Brooklyn who would see my worry and calm my fears. She had a special way of inviting peace in the wake of conflict. Like her dad, Brooklyn is often the first to compromise. She is known by her friends as the mom of the group, facilitating connection and finding solutions to conflicts. As a full-time missionary, Sister Condie is sharing the peace of Christ with the world.

Both of my children have taught me more than I could possibly have offered them. My son, Cameron, has taught me about the power of creativity and shown me what resiliency looks like. He is generous and gifted. I would want to be friends with both of my children if I wasn't their mom. Like every family, we are a combination of our experiences, strengths, weaknesses, and passions. I am so grateful God trusted me to have stewardship over these extraordinary humans. In many ways, I have found healing and heaven as I have mothered them. Brooklyn has had a powerful influence on me in how I see myself, interact with women, and deepen my connection with my Heavenly Mother.

Each of us brings a set of spiritual gifts and superpowers. One of Brooklyn's is definitely her ability to be a peacemaker. Just like the Christlike attributes of meekness and mercy, being known as a peacemaker may not always be praised or lead to a promotion. But as Jesus says in 3 Nephi 12:9, we will be called children of God because of this specific divine characteristic. That is how important peace is to the building of His kingdom.

POINTS TO PONDER

Who do you know that is a peacemaker? Can you surprise them with a batch of cookies or a shout-out on social media this week? Share with them how their gift of peace has helped calm a previous storm.

_____

_____

How do you wake up the Savior in your life to calm storms? List five ways in which you have found connection with the Prince of Peace.

1.

2.

3.

4.

5.

10

BLESSED ARE THEY

Who Are Persecuted for Christ

And blessed are all they who are persecuted for my name's sake, for theirs is the kingdom of heaven. And blessed are ye when men shall revile you and persecute, and shall say all manner of evil against you falsely, for my sake; For ye shall have great joy and be exceedingly glad, for great shall be your reward in heaven; for so persecuted they the prophets who were before you.

—3 NEPHI 12:10–12

Here we are—the beginning of the end, so to speak. The last of the formal blessings of the Book of Mormon Beatitudes is a big one. Jesus is preparing and priming those who may be persecuted. You may feel like the Savior is ending His sermon on a negative note, but don't skip over the blessing. The intended audience is those who are reviled, persecuted, and lied about, in the name of Christ. They will have great rewards. Specifically promised is the gift of joy, gladness, and access to heaven. Jesus compares those who are bullied and harassed, for His name, to the prophets of the past. It may be good company to be found in but doesn't bring much comfort in the moment.

We don't need to look far to find those tormented in the name of faith. The Book of Mormon has some powerhouse examples of persecuted prophets and people. One of my favorites is "Sam the Man," also known as Samuel the Lamanite. The Lord sent Sam to teach and warn. He stood on the wall and prophesied the signs related to both the birth and death of the Savior. But he also warned the people about their possible destruction if they didn't repent (see Helaman 13–16). The Nephites had already threatened to kill the believers. As a child, I used to think that was crazy. Why would someone be killed for believing? Unfortunately, given the cancel culture of the day, it doesn't seem so farfetched anymore.

When Samuel showed up and started sharing his message of sin, signs, and the Savior, the people didn't want to hear any of it and threw him out of the city. Like other heroes, Samuel did not give up. "But behold, the voice of the Lord came unto him, that he should return again, and prophesy unto the people whatsoever things should come into his heart" (Helaman 13:3). Samuel returned to warn and persuade, but this time he stood on the wall of the city. Five years before the birth of the Savior, Sam the Man prophesied that unless they repented, the Nephites would be destroyed.

I am certain Samuel had thoughts of self-doubt and anxiety. Few people heard his forewarnings and admonitions and changed.

> And now, it came to pass that there were many who heard the words of Samuel, the Lamanite, which he spake upon the walls of the city. And as many as believed on his word went forth and sought for Nephi; and when they had come forth and found him they confessed unto him their sins and denied not, desiring that they might be baptized unto the Lord. (Helaman 16:1)

That's good news. But many of the onlookers "did not believe in the words of Samuel [and] were angry with him; and they cast stones at him upon the wall, and also many shot arrows at him as he stood upon the wall" (Helaman 16:2). Arrows, rocks, and angry words don't sound like a great missionary letter to send home to the family. We know that Samuel was ultimately protected from harm, but I am convinced that it wasn't pleasant to stand and shout on a wall and have stones and arrows swooshing by his head.

I love that this Book of Mormon prophet showed us what it looks like to not only be persecuted for his faith but also what it means to not give up. After being kicked out of the city, Sam the Man turned to God and was told to go back. Back to where they didn't like him or want him. I love his resiliency and innovation with plan B up on the wall. And it is wonderful that this willing prophet was able to see that his mission was effective. The message of the Messiah turned hearts back to God. But even with this evidence of success, everyone wasn't a fan. He was literally attacked and abused for this homily.

Being a disciple of Christ means taking upon ourselves His name. This commitment isn't for the faint of heart. Unlike Samuel, we may not be called to declare repentance to an entire city or directed to stand on a wall and prophesy. But when we are baptized, we become His representatives. We are family, and thus we stand up for one another, are loyal, and love when it is difficult. As we prepare for the Second Coming of Christ, we must be prepared for this kind of Book of Mormon opposition to continue.

Elder Delbert L. Stapley compared the wickedness in the Nephites' day to the wickedness in our day:

This account of wickedness and contentions among the Nephites prior to the Lord's birth in the meridian of time is duplicated in the wickedness, contentions, and deceptions of our day as we approach the second coming of our Lord and Savior Jesus Christ. Prophecies concerning these days are also being fulfilled and Satan is stirring up the hearts of men to do iniquity continually; and to thwart, if possible, faith in the great event of Christ's second coming to earth, which I testify is sure to come to pass. Satan is alert and active. We must be more alert and perceptive of the false and insincere schemes of his agents among us.[1]

---

1. Delbert L. Stapley, "Beware of Conspiring Men," https://scriptures.byu.edu/#:t482$24694:c0d61022.

Elder Stapley made this declaration in 1961. It is even more relevant and true of our day. We are fighting a war. Although we know
how it ends, it is hard, scary, and intense. What Jesus taught on the
Sermon on the Mount was relevant then and may be even more criti-
cal today. Sometimes when we are called to fight, we can be strength-
ened knowing who went before us, who stands beside us, and who is
behind us. We are not alone. Angels, prophets, heaven, and priesthood power are with us and enable us to stand up for the cause of
righteousness. It won't be easy, but it will be worth it.

*   *   *

I know many modern-day Sams. People who walk away from
comfortable culture to make eternal covenants. Disciples who share
their faith on social media even when the comment section is filled
with verbal arrows and stones. Young adults and seniors who literally
take Christ's name upon themselves as they put on a black badge and
leave home for faraway lands. But as we consider the last and final
blessing taught by Jesus, the attacks against prophets and people who
choose to stand up publicly to warn and teach are intense and painful.

As you ponder on the principle of persecution, who comes to
mind? I am thinking of a dear friend of mine who is also a public
figure. Videos of some talks he had given surfaced and were extremely
triggering. Social media feedback and backlash seemed to take on a
life of their own. Public opinion was negative and grew angrier by the
day. Those who tried to defend him with posts of their own became
targets themselves. It was painful to watch. Emotions were high, and
he was quickly becoming a story even on local media.

It is easy to vilify others when sitting behind a screen. With just a
swipe, tweet, or post, a person can quickly be cancelled and culturally
crucified. I was watching that happen to someone I cared about and
admired. I knew firsthand how generous he was. How willing he was
to serve the one or sit with the brokenhearted. He let the spirit of the
law influence how he treated others and led this way when in positions
of power. He was willing to hug the people who didn't always deserve
a hug. And he was the first to give grace. He was authentic and real.
He did put on pretenses and didn't take himself too seriously even

when he was noticed in public. My friend was, as the scriptures say, the salt of the earth (see 3 Nephi 12:13).

I am not trying to paint him with a lens of perfection. Like all of us, he had made his share of mistakes and was still learning. But he was not the villain the critics were claiming he was. I had seen his gentle heart in action. He was the kind of friend with whom I knew my name was safe. You know those people who choose to speak well of others when they aren't in the room? Yes, that was my friend. He stood by me when others had spoken disparagingly of me. I had never forgotten how good that felt.

In the wake of the public storm, I remember being asked many times about the true nature of my friend. People knew of our connection and hoped I could explain away what had been said and offer a solution. There was a lot of anger, hurt, and debate. I couldn't speak for him, but I could speak like HIM. Behind all the controversy, he was a person of great faith. He had volunteered and donated years of time in sharing the message of Christ and building His kingdom. This was the person I knew when I thought of and talked of my friend.

What would Jesus say to those who had been hurt by my friend's words? What would Jesus say about my friend? I remember one day, a year after the initial tumult, having a face-to-face conversation with my friend about how he was doing. He tenderly admitted how painful the whole experience had been. I could see on his face that the uproar had taken its toll. No amount of apologizing seemed to help quiet the critics. And he knew it. All he could do was keep going, keep serving, keep learning, and keep trying. I hugged him and reassured him that I knew his heart and promised that he wasn't alone.

The details of this particular situation aren't as essential as understanding the picture of the principle I am hoping to paint. It takes humility and courage to stand up and share our faith. We run the risk of saying too much or not saying it right. We can easily believe the praise of the world and forget in whom we praise. Maybe Jesus was inviting us to be willing to be persecuted because He too had been. To be willing to stand for Him means something.

The Savior admonishes us to stay real and humble because it keeps the door open to being brave when the arrows and stones start flying. Staying grounded, like the salt, keeps us willing. Sam the Man and my friend are not the only ones being asked to stand up and stand firm when stones are thrown. Are you willing to be a disciple of Christ when it isn't popular or fun?

As the sermon closes, Jesus asks if we will take all we have learned and go out and share His teachings. He warns us that it will take guts and gumption. The glory goes to God, and if you are willing to preach and teach of Him, God promises that "ye shall have great joy and be exceedingly glad, for great shall be your reward in heaven" (3 Nephi 12:12).

POINTS TO PONDER

Have you been reviled or persecuted for your faith? What helped you stand on the wall while stones and arrows were shot around you?

_____

_____

_____

_____

_____

_____

Are you a friend who will stand by a friend? Do you keep the names of others safe in the conversations you have?

_____

_____

_____

_____

_____

_____

11

PERFECTION IS POSSIBLE . . .

Eventually

Therefore I would that ye should
be perfect even as I, or your Father
who is in heaven is perfect.

—3 NEPHI 12:48

We have come to the close of the Savior's Sermon on the Mount. The chapter doesn't end with verse 12, but for the purpose of this book, we will stop there. I am sad to have this time with you end. I hope you too have started to see yourself actually sitting with the Savior and being taught in personal ways about becoming like Him. This analysis was never about being overwhelmed or discouraged. It was about learning at His feet and seeing ourselves in the scriptures.

I feel heaven close when I work on any book. But this project has been different in special ways because it has been focused on the words Jesus spoke. And about living like Him because we accept individual invitations. Before we say goodbye, let's jump to the end of the chapter. In the closing verse, Jesus makes a final offering: the invitation to be perfect. To the people of Bountiful, the Savior taught what He had also shared in the New Testament version of the Sermon on the

Mount. But when you compare Matthew 5:48 with 3 Nephi 12:48, you see a significant difference in the wording.

In Matthew, Jesus says, "Be ye therefore perfect, even as your Father which is in heaven is perfect." Does that feel discouraging to read? Maybe it is because we think being perfect means achieving the impossible—checking all the Christian boxes, giving the best *Come, Follow Me* lessons, or never losing our temper. *Perfect* can also be translated from Greek to mean "finished."

As we then look at what the Savior says in the Americas in His second Sermon on the Mount, we understand more clearly the context and command to be perfect. Verse 48 of the chapter says, "Be perfect even as I, or your Father who is in heaven is perfect." Jesus had finished His mortal mission. He had completed what was asked of Him. Christ was perfect when He asked us to eventually be perfect. It means we must complete and finish our mission. We aren't there yet. We aren't complete.

Don't get overwhelmed and discouraged if you are blundering some of the Beatitudes and the blessings haven't yet manifested. Keep practicing the principles. Perfection is possible. It comes eventually.

The more you give heed, believe, are poor in spirit, mourn with those who mourn, and are meek, notice how you feel. Are you feeling more blessed, joyful, and hopeful? Are the everyday worries distracting you from hungering and thirsting after what is right? Consider the mercy you are receiving and how it affects the mercy you offer others. Practice more gratitude to help strengthen the condition of your heart. Celebrate the peacemakers in your family and place of work. And celebrate even the smallest changes you see in yourself. Being a disciple of Christ isn't the easy path, but it is the worthwhile path. You may be persecuted for your faith, but God has promised that any sacrifice we make will be returned with all that He has. As Elder Dieter F. Uchtdorf taught:

> The gospel of Jesus Christ has the answers to all of our problems. The gospel is not a secret. It is not complicated or hidden. It can unlock the door to true happiness. It is not someone's theory or proposition. It does not come from man at all. It springs from the pure and everlasting waters of the Creator of the universe, who

knows truths we cannot even begin to comprehend. And with that knowledge, He has given us the gospel—a divine gift, the ultimate formula for happiness and success.[1]

Pace yourself. Practice one principle at a time. Remember that all is possible through Christ. It is because of Him that we can become like Him. President Dallin H. Oaks taught:

> We are given the scriptures to direct our lives. As the prophet Nephi taught us, we should "feast upon the words of Christ; for behold, the words of Christ will tell you all things what ye should do." Most of the scriptures reporting Jesus's mortal ministries are descriptions of what He did. [This] message today consists of the words of our Savior—what He said.[2]

Sit with the Savior, in a sermon or in your daily scripture reading. Learn of Him. And be with Him. If we accept His invitations, we will be blessed. And perfected, eventually.

---

1. Dieter F. Uchtdorf, "The Way of the Disciple," *Ensign* or *Liahona*, May 2009, 75.
2. Dallin H. Oaks, "The Teachings of Jesus Christ," *Llahona*, May 2023, 102.

About the Author

Ganel-Lyn Condie is a popular motivational speaker and author. As a graduate from Arizona State University with a BS in elementary education and psychology, she became an award-winning journalist and editor of *Wasatch Woman* magazine. Ganel-Lyn is a regular television, podcast, and radio guest. Her talks, books, and media have encouraged people all over the world. Ganel-Lyn's faith and family have helped her learn from all of life's stewardships. Learn more about Ganel-Lyn's work at ganellyn.com by scanning the QR code.